WALKING THE WAY OF SORROWS

Stations of the Cross

Katerina Katsarka Whitley
Original Art by Noyes Capehart

MOREHOUSE PUBLISHING
A Continuum imprint
HARRISBURG · LONDON · NEW YORK

To all those who have suffered and to all those
who are suffering for the sake of Jesus' Name.
—K.K.W.
—N.C.

Text copyright © Katerina Katsarka Whitley
Illustrations copyright © Noyes Capehart

Morehouse Publishing
P.O. Box 1321
Harrisburg, PA 17105

Morehouse Publishing is a Continuum imprint.

The photographs of the woodcuts of the Stations were taken by
Todd Bush, Banner Elk, North Carolina.

Library of Congress Cataloging-in-Publication Data

Whitley, Katerina Katsarka.
Walking the way of sorrows : Stations of the Cross / Katerina Katsarka
Whitley ; illustrations by Noyes Capehart.
p. cm.
ISBN 0-8192-1984-3 (pbk.)
I. Stations of the Cross I. Title.
BX597.S8W55 2004
232.96—DC21

2003011422

Printed in the United States of America
04 05 06 07 08   10 9 8 7 6 5 4 3 2

CONTENTS

PREFACE

My Walk with God

The gift of a creative spirit is one of the real blessings of my life. It is also a great gift, though I didn't always know that. As a young art major, I thought that my visual abilities were fashioned through countless hours of sacrifice, hard work and study. Such thinking certainly fed the notion of the artist as some kind of extraordinary being, precisely the kind of romantic cloak I found so attractive on the shoulders of those artists I had come to admire and emulate.

Following my graduation from Auburn University in 1958, I moved to New York City for what turned out to be one of the great turning points of my life. For three years I worked as a guard and night watchman for the Metropolitan Museum of Art. It was a terribly humbling experience for a cocky young artist like myself to be surrounded each day by the likes of Rembrandt and Rodin, and it was even more deflating to return to my dismal apartment after work and confront the canvas on my easel. From this experience, two things became quite clear to me: (1) I was far from being the artist I wanted and needed to be, and (2) the even more important realization that mortal man cannot take credit for the gift of creative thought and action. I don't know (or remember) if I was ready at that time to give full thanks to God for my talents, but now some forty-three years later there is little doubt in my mind as to the source of my visual curiosity. The fourteen woodcuts now framed and hanging on the walls of The

Church of the Holy Cross in Valle Crucis, North Carolina, and reproduced in this book, were done by my hands, but the spirit that motivated and nourished me throughout this emotional journey came directly from God.

I first proposed the idea for a set of *Stations* to my rector in 1998, but numerous factors side-lined the project, most significantly his unexpected departure from our parish. The concept sat on the proverbial back-burner until a warm morning in May of 2001 when his successor encouraged me to move the simmering pot to the front of the stove. By the time I left his office that morning, I had promised to complete the fourteen woodcuts by Good Friday of 2002.

I did little but think about the project throughout the summer of 2001. Just about the time I began to sharpen my gouges and knives, the dreadful day of September 11 arrived. Like millions of others, my world and its demands seemed of little consequence after the devastation of 9/11. It was a full month before I was able to focus again on the woodcuts. To add to the now mounting sense of urgency in getting the woodcuts under way, my rector asked if it might be possible to have the woodcuts framed and installed in the church by Ash Wednesday.

"But that's a whole month before Good Friday, isn't it?" I asked as a hard knot began to form in my stomach. I glanced at the calendar. Ash Wednesday was approximately sixteen weeks away.

"Well, yes, it is a bit earlier than we'd planned, but I think it would be so special to have them for the start of Lent. That's not a problem, is it?"

What can one say to one's priest at a moment such as this? "A problem? No, no, it's not a problem exactly. It's just . . . just a bit sooner that I'd expected."

Work began on October 14. By the end of that exhausting day, I had my first tangible sketch. Two weeks later I was looking at my first completed woodcut. At this pace, I realized, it would be impossible to complete all fourteen woodcuts and have them framed and installed by April 13.

I completed four woodcuts in November, and five more in December. Of the ten completed woodcuts, however, four were far from satisfying. They had to be re-worked. By this time, I was so completely absorbed with these woodcuts that I did little else but eat and sleep and work on the Stations. The fourteenth and final print was completed on February 3, 2002. With help from two fellow parishioners, the suite of prints was installed in the church sanctuary a scant day before the Ash Wednesday services. And there they still hang. Each Sunday my wife Suzanne and I look at the woodcuts with almost disbelieving eyes. I remember little about the specifics associated with any of the prints. I remember playing certain pieces of music over and over as I cut into the blocks and extracted the images: Mozart's *Requiem* and *Missa Solemnis,* Beethoven's *Symphony No. 9,* Handel's *Messiah,* and John Williams' haunting score for *Schindler's List.* I did everything I could possibly do to charge my small studio with the sense of pathos associated with the Lenten liturgy. Still, it was not my doing that brought these images to life. They just seemed to appear. All I know is that I placed full faith in God's grace to lead me to my solutions. I can't prove to anyone that the Holy Spirit moved through my fingers—and I don't have to—but I know . . . I do know that what I experienced during those sixteen weeks transcended any art-related moments I've ever known. Each day as I worked alone in my studio I felt God's presence and strength. For me, the spiritual feelings that accompanied this journey are indescribable.

I feel very privileged to have been granted this experience. It is my hope now that these images will speak to others, that through the starkness of each picture and Katerina's powerful monologues you will experience a meaningful sense of empathy with the pain and sacrifice of our Savior. Glory to God!

— Noyes Capehart
Boone, North Carolina
May 2003

INTRODUCTION

In 2002, an artist, Noyes Capehart, hung some powerful images of the Stations of the Cross on the walls of the church I attend. After the framed woodcuts of the Stations of the Cross became part of our church, Holy Cross, Valle Crucis, my friend, the artist Noyes Capehart, came to me with an idea that surprised me. Members of our congregation who had helped him in rubbing copies of the Stations' woodcuts had suggested that I write monologues to accompany the Stations. After spending years writing in the voices of biblical women, I found the possibility of entering into the minds of men rather strange. At the time, I was engaged in the writing of another book set in the first century, and I would stop occasionally to contemplate this new avenue of expression, until I started hearing the voice of a Roman soldier who could not get the irenic face of the arrested Jesus out of his mind. So it began.

During Lent 2003 I entered into the darkness surrounding the crucifixion. In the span of two months I wrote the monologues found in this book, trying to think as the Roman and Jewish people of the first century, struggling, both awake and asleep, to understand how human beings could bring themselves to crucify other human beings. It was not a pleasant exercise.

In the course of those same Lenten weeks the bombing and invasion of Iraq was taking place, and I began to inhabit that realm where empathy takes over—putting myself in the place of Iraqi people, especially mothers with children, and even trying to imagine the feelings of the young American soldiers who found themselves in a foreign country as both invaders and conquerors. In that state, I must have been very difficult to live with. I found myself inhabiting both the first and twenty-first centuries that had similarities that frightened and depressed me.

What were the Roman soldiers thinking as they arrested, abused, humiliated, and nailed Jesus to the cross? Were they as cold as the Nazis of the 40s who would put whole families in cattle cars, fully aware that they were sending them to a terrible death? Were they, the Nazis who gunned down innocent people in mass retaliation, and the Romans who drove the nails, *just following orders?* And how does that differ from our own who follow orders by dropping bombs from a distant sky on impersonal targets pinpointed by a computer? What is the difference between close-up killing and long-distance killing? What were they feeling, what were they thinking?

I went through my days teaching classes of young college students, trying to help them look at all aspects of war and the idolatry of patriotism with critical eyes, but I was not getting through to them. Everything was still raw inside them from the sudden fear created by 9/11, which shook the foundations of what they considered their security. I started to understand that fear is at the root of much cruelty.

And I kept writing. In that process, the questions stopped focusing on *them* and started being directed to me. What would I have done had I been a member of that crowd around the cross? What would I have thought about this man Jesus?

I turned to Dorothy L. Sayers again and again and her masterful introduction to her series of plays in *The Man Born to Be King.** And I read aloud her definition of the greatest classical tragic irony of all times: "For the Christian affirmation is that a number of quite commonplace human beings, in an obscure province of the Roman Empire, killed and murdered God Almighty—quite casually, almost as a matter of religious and political routine, and certainly with no notion that they were doing anything out of the way. . . . We, the audience, know what they were doing; the whole point and poignancy of the tragedy is lost unless we realize that they did not. It is in this knowledge by the audience of the appalling truth which is hidden from all the agonists in the drama that the tragic irony consists."

Whenever I read them, these words take my breath away. I try to remember them when I partake of the Holy Eucharist, whenever we reenact this great drama whose "theology locks the whole structure into a massive intellectual coherence," as Sayers explains in the same introduction. We may be aware of the theology, I muse, but do we feel, do we enter into the drama?

It is this vicarious suffering of tragedy, the shock of recognition, the thrill of being there, that I wanted to experience through my monologues. We talk of the crucifixion, we partake of "the body and blood" of the crucified, but do we enter into the agony and pain of it? Do we allow ourselves to *enter* into the drama?

As I wrote this book, I began to understand the desire of the mystics to experience the physical pain, to see the stigmata on their hands and feet. For the first time I understood something about Saint Francis of Assisi and Santa Teresa of Avila, and others. And I began to comprehend also why the Stations of the Cross have become so important to so many believers through the centuries. It is not enough to say the words and grasp some of them intellectually; every now and then we need the shock of entering into the agony of the Garden of Gethsemane and of the Cross. For we all abandon Jesus as Peter and James and John did in order to rest, in order not to feel. We all become indifferent to him as were the passersby on the Via Dolorosa. We all understand something of the cruelty of those who just follow orders in inflicting pain. And we all have practiced injustice.

But also, we too feel the longing of the woman who wiped his brow, the grief of the lamenting, inconsolable women of

Jerusalem, the wonder and awe of the centurion; and we too suddenly recognize the presence of the Holy as Simon of Cyrene did.

I am probably wrong in ascribing a vestige of humanity to each of the characters who were involved in the act of the crucifixion, but I cannot believe in a totally evil human being. And I keep remembering: they didn't know what they were doing.

But we do know. May God have mercy on us all as we enter into these stories allowing them to cause us to feel pain, hope, love, and gratitude. Assume the persona of each one of them on the way of sorrows as you walk with them. Read these monologues aloud to yourself or to each other. Use them for personal or group meditation. Take the time needed to become a part of the story. Don't rush through Lent and Holy Week. Enter into the darkness of the crucifixion. It is only by fully entering into and living in the darkness that you can truly recognize the Light of Easter.

— Katerina Katsarka Whitley
May 2003

*Sayers, Dorothy L. *The Man Born to Be King.* Grand Rapids: William B. Eerdmans Publishing Company, 1974, pages 5–6.

STATION I

Jesus Is Condemned to Death

As seen by the arresting soldier

Jesus Is Condemned to Death

*Then Pilate took Jesus and had him flogged. And the
soldiers wove a crown of thorns and put it on his head,
and they dressed him in a purple robe.* John 19:1–2.

Surprised at feeling no resistance from the prisoner, I
turned to look at him but, like a fool, happened to
glance at his eyes.

How I wish I hadn't done that. How I wish I hadn't seen
his eyes. I had to turn away from him. We Romans are a hard
lot, but I could not stand to look at his face. And don't you
dare think me soft! I have brought many criminals before
Pilate in my year here in this dump called Jerusalem and didn't
flinch for a moment when I did it. I felt satisfaction when
Pilate's meanness hit at them and his disdain made them want
to crawl away. But this prisoner had me baffled from the start.
I dragged him into the praetorium's main hall and felt no resistance from him. It was as if he was coming with me willingly,
but how can this be? *Look* at him. Even with that ridiculous
crown of thorns on his head, there is nothing of the martyr in
him. Why isn't he resisting me? It would make it so much easier on me if he did.

I am so used to their hatred, it slips right off me, leaves me
untouched. I am so used to their anger and the arrogance of
the Jews who look at us as if we are worms—even when we
lord it over them—that I have learned to spit it right back at
them. But this one. . . . The strange thing is that he too is a
Jew, yet there is no arrogance in him. This is the funny thing,
scary, to tell you the truth: I heard someone whisper that he
really *is* a king in disguise. Oh, yeah, I said, that will really go

over well with Pilate. And Tiberius will love it! Those bastards in the palace kill each other for a glance—imagine hearing that a Jew is a secret king.

So I laughed it off. What else could I have done? But then the fates cursed me, and I turned and looked at the prisoner's face to see why he was making it easy for me to drag him to Pilate—that's all. He was exhausted by then. I could tell he had been up all night, dragged from one hypocrite to the other—that snake Caiaphas who sent him to Pilate, who then sent him to that fox Herod, and now here he is again, standing before the hyena, Pilate. I hate all of them for lording it over us when *we* do all the work, *we* slave to make them rich, to keep them powerful. I hate them. So when I turned around to look at the prisoner—Jesus, they call him—I expected to see the same hatred in *him*. I hadn't heard anything bad about the man, so I figured he must really be furious to be treated so roughly. And that was my mistake. I turned, and he was looking full at me. His eyes, huge and sad, stayed on me, and at that moment, with a sharp pain that stopped my breath, I remembered my mother's eyes the first time she saw me kick another child. Love and sadness, I thought, love and sadness. I wanted to turn away, to stop looking at him, but he wouldn't let me. He urged his love on me, he urged it, I tell you. I wanted to kick him then, I couldn't stand it. But I pushed him ahead of me as rough as I could, and he stumbled for a moment but didn't fall. He turned one more time and looked at me, full in the eyes as before and, I'm ashamed to say, he saw my tears. I said without speaking, "It's not you, it's my mother," but he seemed to hear me clearly, and then he continued into the cold hall and stood quietly before Pilate.

The fates took over again and made me stare from him to Pilate, and what I saw didn't make me feel good about my people. There are times I hate that I am a Roman and a soldier, and then I hate Pilate all the more. Look at him now. Sitting there like some man of great worth passing judgment on this dignified Jew whose eyes are loving like a mother's. Gods of the Pantheon, how I hate what we are doing.

But look at his own people, look at *them!* They are out for blood. So what makes them different from us? Hatred is hatred no matter who is feeling it, right? Hey, that's good. My old tutor's words are rushing back to me after such a long time. What is this? Why am I suddenly remembering the only two good people in my life—my mother and my tutor? What is causing all this? Is it the prisoner? What is it about him, what is it?

Maybe that young man—the one with tears in his eyes—maybe he knows. He must be one of his followers. They say the prisoner had many friends, devoted followers. Where are the creatures now?

I approach the weeping young man, but he turns away. He never takes his eyes off the man Jesus; he acts as if he'll die if he loses sight of him, even for a minute. "Hey," I whisper, "hey there, you Jew. What is it about your friend, what is it that makes him so calm, so self-possessed?"

"He's the only one here who is not afraid," the man whispers, but he breaks down sobbing, and I can't afford to talk to him again. Pilate is looking at me. I would like to make a rude gesture, but I'm not ready to die.

I have to find out what happens next. Pilate, the hyena with red eyes, is playing his favorite game again. I have heard him rant and rave against the Jews, but look, see how he's falling into their hands to do the bidding of the high priests who fill his pockets with their gold, stolen from their own people? Damn them, damn them all.

What is it about the prisoner? What? His friend must be right. All of us are trembling with fear inside, no matter that we Romans hold the whip and the power. He is the only one who is not afraid. What do I do now?

Let us pray:

Lord Jesus Christ, you faced humiliation and torture without complaining.

Be with us in the hours of trial.

Lord Jesus Christ, you faced arrest and death without fear.

Be with all those who are afraid today.
Be with all those who are tortured and treated
unjustly in many parts of the world.

Lord Jesus Christ, as on the day of your arrest and flogging, much evil against the innocent is perpetrated by people who think they are doing God's will.

Forgive them and us for our sin.

Kyrie eleison.

Christé eleison.

Kyrie eleison.

STATION II

Jesus Takes Up His Cross

As seen by a woman passing by

Jesus Takes Up His Cross

"Which of these three, do you think, was a neighbor to the man who fell into the hands of the robbers?" [The lawyer] said, "The one who showed him mercy." Jesus said to him, "Go and do likewise." Excerpt from Luke 10:25–37

When I saw him with that cross on his back, I almost dropped the baby. This is what it comes to, I thought—our life is for nothing after all. This warm, sweet-smelling baby in my arms, this tender little helpless thing I'm holding, one day may end up like him. Carrying a cross. Oh, God of Abraham, Jacob, and Moses, what fate awaits all our sons in this occupied land?

It's not even *my* baby—it's my daughter's. But she died giving birth, so here I am learning to mother a little one again. When I saw the condemned man pass by my door, alone and burdened, blood running down his face, a cruel crown of thorns on his hair, I held on to the baby and ran outside. All I could think of was—someone should be near him at a time like this. With the Romans' thirst for blood, punishing us just for being Jews, I didn't ask, "What has the man done to deserve this?" I've heard it said they kill for sport, these Romans. So I walked alongside him for a while, thinking he needs another body near him, poor man, poor man. He needs his mother at a time like this—but there was nobody with him when the Romans pushed him out into our street. There was a crowd in the distance, but that's different—a body needs another body near him. That's all. Like this baby here. If I let it go, it will die. It needs to be close to me to live.

But he, the man under the burden of the cross, is going to die. I hold life, he holds death. That's how it is in this world, isn't it? It's too much to bear at times, knowing that we all must die. But to die on a cross? What evil mind thought that one up?

Underneath the yells of the soldiers behind us, the wailing of women in the distance, the curses of angry men close by, I hear his murmur. It's like a prayer, I think, and I strive to listen. "Abba," he is crying, "my father!" Who is his father? says I to the baby, Who is his father? Let's go find him and bring him here! But the baby doesn't answer. And then it comes to me, and it stops me like a terror. I've heard this voice before, I've heard these same words before. He always called God his Father, that rabbi who walked around with his many friends, his hundreds of followers. That nice rabbi, that strong young man who spoke everywhere giving us hope. What was his name? Teacher, they called him. What else? What was his name?

Someone comes from behind and grabs me by the arm to stop me from walking next to the condemned man. I turn to see my cousin, the Levite. "You have no business here," he says, "next to a criminal."

I pull my arm free. "Doesn't the Lord ask us to have compassion for the stranger?" I ask. "But tell me, who is he? What is the condemned man's name?"

"Don't you remember?" he asks. "Have you forgotten the story you heard him tell, the one that made fun of me, a Levite?"

It hits me hard, I tell you, hard, for I remember it all too well. That good man who told such stories, ah, such stories! I had been passing by that day, saw the crowds, and stopped to listen. Someone asked the young rabbi, "And who is my neighbor?" and the teacher started: "A man was going down from Jerusalem to Jericho . . ." and continued with the story I have never forgotten. How the traveler was beaten up by thieves and left to die. A priest and then a Levite passed by and ignored his hurt, but a *Samaritan* who saw him took pity on him and nursed him and then carried him to a place of rest and paid for all his care. . . . How angry my cousin and all his friends had been when they heard that story!

And now here is the storyteller suffering worse than the man in his parable. What can one do? I see the wailing women coming closer and someone says, "There is his mother!" So I drop back to let those who love him walk closer to him. I turn to my cousin and yell, furious now. "Did you have something to do with this? Did you? Did you and your friends go to the high priest and to the Romans to speak against him? Were you afraid of his truth?"

The Levite's silence deafens me. I hold the baby closer, and with slow steps turn back for home. What will happen to this baby when he grows up? What use is there trying to obey God when good men, like the rabbi who spoke God's truth, are being dragged to their miserable death?

Let us pray:

Lord, we are all saddened and terrified and angry
   when we see oppression and injustice.

Have mercy on the oppressed and their oppressors.

Forgive us our self-righteousness.

Forgive us our ease and comfort while others struggle
   in turmoil.

*Help us to recognize those who are merciful even when
   the world despises them.*

Help us to recognize kindness in those we consider
   unworthy.

Forgive us the sin of pride.

Forgive us our hardened hearts.

Kyrie eleison.

Christé eleison.

Kyrie eleison.

STATION III

Jesus Falls the First Time

As seen by John bar-Zebedee

Jesus Falls the First Time

This is the disciple who is testifying to these things and has written them, and we know that his testimony is true. John 21:24

How can I even begin to speak of it? I cannot go beyond the sorrow that fills me and chokes me and makes me unable to describe it in words. If I could stop thinking about it all the time, maybe then I would have the ability to utter it.

I was his favorite friend—they all thought it and many times said so aloud, but in derision, and even jealousy. If I was his favorite, I was also the biggest coward of them all. I did follow close behind during the bogus trials. I never left him with my eyes. They at least stayed with him—my eyes, filled with tears as they were, filled with the sorrow of what had befallen him—my teacher, my friend, the best human being ever to walk this earth. That's how I saw him from the very beginning.

But I was also ambitious and wanted him to succeed so I could succeed with him. There is a difference there. James and I wanted to be his helpers, but when we asked him to remember us and make us his number one assistants, his astonishment and disappointment in us were blistering. We never got over it, James and I. The rest were furious at us for our ambition and gall, but it was his immense sorrow that hit us between the eyes. He looked at us and asked, in that quiet voice of his that cut through everything superfluous and moved straight to the heart of every question: "You do not know what you are asking. Can you drink the cup that I drink?" and his eyes

burned me. By then I was shaking. "Yes," I lied, and knew I
was lying, to my abiding shame. Yes, though I knew immediately that I couldn't, not then, not then. But now it is coming,
and I am willing to share in his pain and in his disappointment. If I only had been able to share his abandonment.

I know I am going on and on and you have no idea what
I'm talking about. The scene you asked me to describe—that's
the most painful one I remember before the hammer and the
nails. The Romans had burdened him with the cross and he,
being already tired, having been up all night—first the sorrowful goodbye to us, then the agonizing hours of prayer in the
garden, then the betrayal and that shameful dragging him from
Caiaphas to Pilate, to Herod and back to Pilate—all that had
worn him out. He had a tendency to disregard his physical
exhaustion, but never the one of the spirit. He always managed to find a little time to be alone, to pray, to listen to his
Father, as he put it. But that day, the physical agony seemed to
be overwhelming. He could hardly stand up. I thought the
other *agon*, the struggle of his spirit, he had already conquered
in Gethsemane.

He seemed to be the only one not afraid, even though so
much evil was directed at him. But then they put that heavy
burden of the tree on him, and his back, already torn from the
whip, couldn't take it. He stumbled and fell.

I started to run to him, to take it from him, to lift him up,
but James held me back. He said through his own tears, his
face paler than I had ever seen it, his hand strong in its grip
but trembling violently, he said to me, "John, the Master told
us not to get ourselves arrested. He said this was his burden
alone. He wants us safe for his own reasons. I forbid you to
disobey him."

"But, James," I cried, "James, we abandoned him in the
garden. One of us must go to help him now."

James then took his eyes from the fallen figure of our best
and dearest and said to me so sadly that it hurt my broken
heart even more, "John, he especially asked me to protect you.
'Your time will come,' he said to me, 'but it is not now. See

that John is safe,' and I had to promise, John, I did." I heard a sob escape from my brother, and I knew he always told me the truth. But I still believe I should have gone to my fallen friend, my Master and my Lord.

They led him away, and we followed, we the cowards, we, his dearest friends. The crowds pushed and surged, but I was determined to stay with him, even though the way was hard beyond measure for him, and seeing him in that state was more than my eyes could bear. But I kept following, and the image of his falling under the burden of the cross has burned itself in my mind. So much has happened since then, but that terrible walk of sorrows stays with me always.

Now my time has come to walk the way of sorrow for his sake. I am ready. I have relived those terrible hours in Jerusalem in telling you about them, but my heart is light and free for myself. I will soon see my friend again. How his love has sustained me all these many years, how close I have felt his presence even though all our early friends are gone now. We abandoned him in the garden, but we all have stayed with him ever since. And as he told us, each one of us who has followed in his footsteps has known physical agony. It was only proper. We have been grateful for the honor. "My children," he told us on that last sorrowful night, "my children, I will not leave you comfortless." And he has not. Praise God he has not.

Yes, I am ready.

Let us pray:

Oh, God, you allowed your beloved Son to know the sorrow of humanity out of your great love for those you have created.

Help us to trust in your love even when we stumble and fall.

Lord, whether our days are few, like those of your servant James, or many, like those of your servant

John, help us to be ready when you call us to
yourself.

And teach us how to carry each other's burdens.

Fill us with the love and loyalty of your beloved
apostle.

*Let our hearts burn within us whenever we draw away
from you.*

Bless both our joys and our tears.

Kyrie eleison.

Christé eleison.

Kyrie eleison.

STATION IV

Jesus Meets His Afflicted Mother

As told by Mary of Nazareth

Jesus Meets His Afflicted Mother

And the child's father and mother were amazed at what was being said about him. Then Simeon blessed them and said to his mother Mary, "This child is destined for the falling and the rising of many . . . and a sword shall pierce your own soul too." Luke 2:33–35.

he crowd finally made way and the soldiers let me through. Even they have mothers, I thought, and maybe somewhere under the helmets the memory of a mother still has a place, and under that fancy Roman dress a heart still beats with remembered love. "He is my son," I cried, "my child; let me through." And they did.

Jesus was still carrying the cross on his torn back, on the shoulders that used to be so strong before they slashed them with their horrid whip. He stopped and faced me when, mad with grief, I ran through the crowd calling his name. "Yeshua, my child!" He made an effort to push the shameful cross from his back to the side, but as mothers do, I looked at him carefully and saw the wounds, even though he tried to shield me from them. On his back I saw under the torn folds of his cloak how the blood had seeped through and how raw his exposed shoulder looked. He turned so we would be face-to-face.

"And a sword shall pierce your own soul too," old Simeon had said. Now, reaching out to my son, bloodied and sorrowful as he was on the road to Golgotha, I had a vision of the long-ago presentation visit to the Temple. I saw Simeon's face of wonder again and heard Anna's ecstatic joy as the words poured out from their aged throats—"I have seen thy salvation, oh, Lord." And I saw my own face as I must have been then, so young, so filled with joy unspeakable, my arms, with that sweet baby weight in them filling them, my arms stretching out to hand my child to Simeon whose old eyes were weeping—"Let thy servant now depart in peace, oh God, for my eyes have seen thy salvation." And I saw the young girl, the mother I was then turning to Joseph with such delight and saying to him, "Do you understand what they are saying?" but I was also thinking something else I would not reveal to him: "This is my own darling child, Joseph. Make them stop. Let me enjoy him, please. Tell them not to fill me with foreboding."

Those young arms of mine were suddenly emptied of the sweet warmth of baby flesh, and there I was, an old woman now, stretching them trembling to my grown son, the stranger he had become these last few years. "Old Simeon was right, my son," I whispered when he took my hands and held me in a way that kept me from touching his back, from feeling the blood on the open wounds. He didn't need to ask what I meant; he always understood me, many times before I opened my mouth. "How often," he whispered to me alone, "I have longed to keep you from this pain." And that broke me.

It had taken me so long to understand that he could not be like the others, the children who stayed close by, who belonged to me. I, who had heard the angels' song at his birth, who had believed in the promises, who had said *Yes* to Gabriel, I found it so hard to accept his going away on the road that would lead to this, the walk of sorrows. "I know, son," I told him now. "I know Someone else was calling you all the time. But how I have missed you."

His eyes were full of sorrow—for me, for the hostile crowd, for his friends, for the whole world. How could we possibly enter into such sorrow? And how could I keep from remembering? That night in Bethlehem was with me, taunting me, the music and the star, the angels and the promise, the hope of salvation. Was I crying them aloud, these memories of early joy? Where is peace, my son, I was crying inside, where is the promised peace?

He looked all around and then back at me. "The peace of God," he said quietly; "I give it to you, Mother, but not as the world gives it . . ." and memories of his words through the years filled my mind. His dreams were always different from ours, his truth eluded us. "Is this the world's doing then?" I asked him wanting to know now, urgently, as if everything depended on it.

He gave my hand one last pressure. "Because of the Father, I have overcome the world," he told me, and I heard behind the words the unspoken understanding: "Despite all this, I have overcome the world." There was no irony there. I believed him. I touched his face one last time and then the Romans pulled me away. Even they managed not to be too rough. I was the mother after all. And this prisoner, this torn and bleeding young man, was my son. "I have overcome the world." How they would laugh if they heard him. But I walked away repeating his words, and everyone who heard me thought I had gone mad.

But now I was sane.

Let us pray:

For our mothers and our fathers, Lord, we offer
thanks.

For those who gave us birth and nurtured us;

For those who have become mothers and fathers in
our journey through life's many byways;

For strangers who offered us food to nourish our bodies;

For those who, offering their gifts of knowledge,
taught us;

*For those who shared with us their faith with your
mercy;*

For all these mothers and fathers, we offer our thanks,
oh, God.

For Mary, the mother of Jesus,

For the young girl who said *Yes* to God's messenger,

For the mother who had her doubts later, and for the broken mother who held him as he was dying,

We offer our eternal gratitude to you, oh Father of our Jesus the Christ.

Kyrie eleison.

Christé eleison.

Kyrie eleison.

STATION V

The Cross Is Laid on Simon of Cyrene

As told by Simon to his sons

The Cross Is Laid on Simon of Cyrene

They compelled a passer-by, who was coming in from the country, to carry his cross; it was Simon of Cyrene, the father of Alexander and Rufus. Mark 15:21.

I never want to see the place again, but you may go back, my sons, the brothers will need you. I hold the memory of it with pain, because of all that happened, even though that one day has proved the most important one in my life. . . .

I was coming back from tilling the field, you see, and heard the noise, a roar like that of the lions and other beasts I used to hear back home in Cyrene, deep and fearful, with sudden ugly yelps and screams, a sound I hated and thought I had forgotten. The roar of predators after a victim. I came to the edge of the city center and looked up the narrow street, saw the Romans cursing and shoving the crowds back, saw the Jews of the city whispering, some rubbing their hands with glee, others standing aloof as if none of the dirt could touch them, some with their heads hanging down, ashamed, I thought. I was a big man back then and the crowd made way for me.

What's all the commotion? I thought, but I must have said it aloud, because one of the Romans looked at me and nudged another. "Here," he said, "look at this dark one. They are strong, these Africans. Let's make him do it." I felt my anger rising. You fools, I wanted to shout, can you not tell that I am a man of Cyrene, but a Jew nonetheless? I had no idea what it was they had in mind for me, but they came from behind and pushed me forward. The crowd, seeing the Romans, again

27

made way. I lifted my arms to strike, as I had always done in a
tight spot—strike before they strike you was my motto—ready
to push my hands in their faces but there, in front of me, I saw
a man down on his knees, a heavy rough-hewn tree crushing
his back. I stared at his bleeding back, then turned to the
Romans to curse them. One of them pointed to the heavy tree.
"You, dark one," he ordered, "pick up that cross. The prisoner
is weak."

I was horrified. A cross? How could I, a Jew, pick up a
cross? The shame of it would never leave me. Should I run?
Should I fight? "No," I cried out, "no." But at that moment
the man on the ground made an effort to stand up and, as he
struggled, he turned his head to look at me and my tormen-
tors. I saw a face covered with blood. "My son," he whispered,
"give me a hand," and tried again to regain his footing.
Instinctively I reached my arm to steady him and, as I did, I
felt his muscles and was surprised. "My son?" I questioned,
"but you're as young as I." "God's blessings on you," he said
again, quietly, to me alone, as if there was not a whole crowd
roaring nearby. I was angry enough to kill. "What have they
done to you?" I asked and heard my voice breaking. "I'll kill
the murderers, I will!" He closed his eyes for a moment as if
withdrawing, saying *No* to my passion. "Never," he said to me
alone, "never repay violence with violence."

Bewildered, I stared at him. "Why," I asked, "why?" He
looked at me, and it was just he and I there amidst the throng;
everyone else had disappeared. I bent and grabbed the heavy
cross. I wanted to swing with it and hit everyone in its path,
hit them hard until they dropped. But he too was close by, and
I couldn't hurt him. I saw that he would never run to escape
my fury. So I bent and lifted the cross on my back, and he
reached his bleeding hand and closed his fingers on my arm in
gratitude, just for a moment. And through me ran his love.

I hear your questions, my son Rufus. I see your tears, my
son Alexandros. But that is what happened. I felt his love run
through me, and I was changed. I trudged ahead, he at my
side. "Who are you, friend?" I asked him. "What have you

done to deserve this?" "The Father is in me, and I am in the Father," he said, as if talking to himself. "They would have no power over me if it had not been given them from above." I understood nothing, praying he'd go on talking to me, but his strength was ebbing. We trudged on in sorrow, oblivious to all the others.

We had stopped saying words, but we were still talking to each other. I asked, and he responded. So it was that my life changed. I couldn't endure what came next. Like a coward I ran away and watched from afar. And as you heard from our brother Peter and the others, I was not the only coward. But that didn't make it any better. I think I spent the following days crying to God, until I came upon another crowd and stood by the portico of the Temple to hear Peter's voice ringing out, the Galilean accent unmistakable. ". . . this man," he was saying, "handed over to you according to the definite plan and foreknowledge of God, you crucified and killed by the hands of those outside the law. But God raised him up . . ." and I felt my heart cracking inside me. I knew he was talking about the crucified man I had helped and then abandoned. I waited that day to talk to Peter, and the rest you know. I have not moved away from that man of sorrows again, and vowed to return to my native land to tell others about him.

But you, my sons, you don't have my painful memories. You may return to the land where he walked under the burden of the cross. You may walk again that Via Dolorosa, as I have come to think of it; but as you do, remember to thank God, remember.

Let us pray:

Lord Jesus, long have we sinned before your eyes.

We have looked at people's skin, instead of their hearts.

We have sinned against your children, those who look different from us.

Oftentimes we have taken advantage of those who were born in other lands.

We have looked down on the poor, the dispossessed, and the immigrants.

We have not always honored those who do hard manual labor; instead of praising them, we have despised them.

We offer our thanks for your servant Simon, who took up your cross to lighten your burden.

May we so live that our labor will be blessed,

And your burden of mercy and pain for this suffering world will be lifted according to the ability and faithfulness of all those who strive to do your will.

Kyrie eleison.

Christé eleison.

Kyrie eleison.

STATION VI

A Woman Wipes the Face of Jesus

As told by Veronica

A Woman Wipes the Face of Jesus

He had no form or comeliness that
we should look at him,
and no beauty that
we should desire him.
He was despised and rejected
by men;
a man of sorrows
and acquainted with grief . . . Isaiah 53:2b–3a (RSV)

ome, come, I'll show you the place. This is the window from where I first saw him. You see up there, above this narrow climbing path? It's on the second story. I used to spend my scarce free moments looking out, seeing the life of the city pass me by.

I worked for one of the big-name priests—I won't tell you his name. It doesn't matter now. I have forgiven him. He used to have me whipped when I disobeyed him. That day, nothing else entered my mind but to run down to that man of sorrows. I didn't even consider what would happen to me afterwards.

Look, you see how the road climbs up, so narrow and so tortuous? Imagine having to climb it with a tree on your back. From the distance, I saw the procession stop, and the Romans forced another man to carry it. But when I got close to Jesus later, I saw that he had been beaten nearly to death already. I didn't ask, "What has the man done?" I only knew that he reminded me of someone.

You see, the priest used to read Isaiah aloud to himself. I heard him all over the house. Wherever I was and whatever I was doing, there was his booming voice, reading aloud. And though he thought me stupid like a woman (that's what he used to say), I learned everything by heart. I was like a sponge in those days. I couldn't read, but I memorized what I heard and said it over and over to myself when I lay down and tried to rest my aching limbs.

On that day, I heard the roar and the ugly noise from afar. The priest had gone to his temple duties, so I took a breather and leaned out the window. And what I saw made me sick and brought to mind the words I had memorized:

He was wounded for our transgressions,
  he was bruised for our iniquities . . .
He was oppressed, and he was afflicted,
  yet he opened not his mouth . . .

There he is, I cried, the man of sorrows. There was a crowd ahead of him and many more trailing behind. The ones in front were Roman soldiers, mostly bored and indifferent. On their faces I could read: We're all out for blood, Romans and Jews alike. And they were right, I think. On the faces of those Jews who were jeering at the prisoner I could see the same thirst for blood. But behind the man of sorrows there were others— men bent over, hiding their faces, and women openly weeping.

I ran down the stairs as I was. I needed to be near him, to offer him what comfort I could. I emerged from the doorway, and it was at that moment he was passing by me. Suddenly he seemed to me to be all alone. Everyone else did not matter; I could not even hear their noise. I saw his face, torn, bleeding, sad beyond human understanding. Dust and sweat had mingled on his brow together with fresh and dried blood. I had a clean cloth in my hand. I must have just picked it up to do some dusting but had not used it. It still smelled clean from the sun and air.

There was no moment to stop, to think before doing. I reached up and wiped his ravaged face. A simple thing, isn't that so? I had wiped many children's faces in my years of service. But this was different. This face was all eyes, and the eyes held a grief not known to other men. It was just he and I—a man who was hurt and a woman who knew about pain. And then he passed on by. All of a sudden I was no longer alone. The crowd closed in on me, and then I saw my master, the priest. He looked furious. All I could think of was, What a different face from that of the man of sorrows! We are all descendants of Abraham, the rabbis tell us, but what a difference between us, eh? One, a face of grief unspeakable, without anger or bitterness, the other, a face of hate and fury. How can these two be related? my simple mind wondered. The priest was yelling at me, and then I stopped thinking, so I could hear him.

"How dare you?" he asked. "Who gave you permission to give comfort to a prisoner?"

"Is that what I did?" I asked, still in a kind of dreamy state, holding that precious bloody cloth in my hands.

"Get out!" he yelled. "Gather your miserable things and leave."

I shrugged. I didn't possess anything of value, except this cloth in my hands, so I followed the procession, his angry voice following me. But I was now among the weeping women and all I heard was their sounds of grief. I decided to stay with them and join my tears with theirs.

Years have gone by since then. I certainly did not keep the cloth with his blood and sorrow as any kind of relic! Our people have been forbidden from seeing God in things, certainly not in anything as humble as a cleaning cloth. But others have wanted to know about it. They are mostly Greeks and Romans, people who have always made images of their gods, I am told, and they told me not to wash the cloth, not to discard it, to keep it because now it is miraculous. But what I think is—I keep it because it reminds me of the one I call the man of sorrows. If others see his image on it, that is fine with me. For me, it means he shares my loneliness and all my sorrows. I have learned much about him since that day.

Someday, we'll talk about those good memories. For now, it is enough that I was privileged to offer him just a moment of comfort. That is all.

Let us pray:

Merciful Christ, you have known the sorrow of this earth's humble people.

We remember this hour those who have labored for others:

Cleaning women and other servants, those who have scrubbed streets and latrines and those who have scrubbed houses.

We remember those who have wiped the tears of others:

Mothers and grandmothers, nurses, and the slaves of old.

We remember those who left their own children behind in order to tend to the hurts of other people's children.

Forgive us for neglecting the humble, for forgetting those who have served us, for not honoring the work of servanthood and mercy.

Kyrie eleison.

Christé eleison.

Kyrie eleison.

STATION VII

Jesus Falls the Second Time

As seen by James bar-Zebedee

Jesus Falls the Second Time

*Holy Father, protect them in your name those that you
have given me, so that they may be one, as we are one.
While I was with them, I protected them in your name,
those that you have given me. I guarded them, and not
one of them was lost . . .* John 17:11b–12a

And 15: *I am not asking you to take them out of the
world, but I ask you to protect them from the evil one.*

he first time he fell, I could hardly control John, my
brother. He was the youngest among us and Jesus'
dearest friend. The arrest, which we both followed
closely, had already destroyed John. Because of our connection
to the priestly family, we had easy access to the courts where
they dragged the Master that night. We moved with the crowd,
despising ourselves for not speaking out. John wept the whole
time; he was unable to stop. I wanted to lash out, but Jesus
had forbidden us from interfering. I kept hearing his voice—
the voice that rarely rang with irony, but this time I noticed it
when they arrested him. He looked at the crowd of the Temple
police, and what I saw on his face when they rushed at him
was a look that said, If only they knew. Then, when they laid
their hands on him, so many of them against one unarmed
teacher standing still—not giving any resistance—I heard his
voice, and had I not known him so well, I would have thought
he was mocking them. He said, "Did you come to arrest me
with violence? Do you not know that I could have called
legions from heaven to defend me?" Did they know? Did they
suspect?

But when Peter, crazed with grief, drew a knife and attacked one of the servants, Jesus looked at him as if to say, "Peter, you still don't understand. You still don't know that the way of violence is not my way." I knew that he didn't want us to defend him but that he wanted us to trust him, as always; and we had let him down again and again and again. I was sick of our fecklessness. I knew then that I was going to obey from that moment on. I also knew his concern for John, my sometimes hot-headed and other times tender younger brother. So I followed John everywhere he went.

After Jesus fell the first time under the weight of the cross, I had to restrain John. From then on he was a wreck; like his beloved master, John could barely stand up, but he was not going to leave him without his presence, ineffectual though it was. The others had dispersed but, occasionally, in that mixed up throng, I had glimpses of the women. Their sorrow was more than I could bear to see, so I avoided them.

I saw Jesus fall the second time and stepped directly in front of John so he couldn't see. This time the women surged forward wailing and, before the Romans could stop them, they were lifting him up. I recognized Mary Magdalene among them and Joanna, whose husband was in Herod's court. She must have said something to the Romans, for they did not interfere. One of the soldiers held up the tree while the women stretched their hands to lift the fallen Jesus. He spoke to them and they to him, but no one else could hear what they were saying. Jesus then reached his bleeding hands and touched each one of them briefly, and then the women withdrew quietly, their eyes on him, imploring him.

"They can't understand why he is not saving himself," I heard John's voice saying in my ear and, startled, I knew that I had forgotten all about him. I turned to him. His lips were trembling like those of a little child. "He saved everyone else who came to him," John went on as if begging me to understand. "Why is he not saving himself?"

I remembered then with a clarity that stopped my breath and I bent in two because of my chest pain. John, frightened for me now, leaned toward me. "Don't you remember?" I whispered. "He told us why." And memories flooded my mind. I could hear his voice clearly just a day or so before saying, ". . . unless a grain of wheat falls into the earth and dies, it remains just a single grain. But if it dies, it bears much fruit." And that repeated image he brought before us that made no sense then, when he was with us so vibrant and alive: ". . . so must the Son of Man be lifted up that you may have eternal life . . ."

I said to John, "Do you remember all the times he told us he must be lifted up to draw everyone to himself?" And John nodded, unable to speak. I said to him, rather severely I'm afraid, "John, pull yourself together. The Master will not perform any miracle this time. He will not save himself. He is obeying the will of his Father."

Then John wiped his tears, stood up straighter, and said quietly, "James, I will stay with him to the end. You go get some rest." The word sounded so alien to my ears—rest. Why would I want to rest when the best of us, the holy one, was in such agony before my eyes?

I said to John, "I slept last night, when I should have stayed awake. I will not rest, until the end comes." And we continued together, watching from afar.

Let us pray:

Oh, God, through the ages, you have protected your own.

We thank you for the promises given to the disciples and to us.

The terrors of the night encircle us and we sleep, forgetting to stay awake and pray.

The spirit is willing but the flesh is weak.
Forgive us, Lord.

We thank you for James, one of the first martyrs to the faith.

We thank you for all those who gave up their lives
   when they refused to betray your name.

Give us the same strength and courage.

Help us to watch and pray.

Kyrie eleison.

Christé eleison.

Kyrie eleison.

STATION VIII

Jesus Meets with the Women of Jerusalem

As seen by Joanna

Jesus Meets with the Women of Jerusalem

*But Jesus turned to them and said, "Daughters of
Jerusalem, do not weep for me, but weep for yourselves
and for your children, for the days are surely coming
when they will say, 'Blessed are the barren, and the
wombs that never bore, and the breasts that never
nursed . . .'"* Luke 23:28–29

So when they reached the city gate without stopping
but continued toward Golgotha, we knew that the
end was close at hand and no hope remained. There
are times when the Romans show mercy, and this is the place
where they release the prisoner—at the gate. It is capricious
mercy at best, or so it seems to us, but we still call it mercy.
We waited, our collective breath suspended, our loud weeping
suppressed, praying for their mercy, but it did not arrive. They
pressed on, and we knew then that this was the end, that Jesus
would not escape crucifixion.

A loud wail rose and reached everyone's ears. How many
of us were there? I remember seeing his mother, at least two of
his aunts, and the mother of James and John, and there was
the Magdalene, of course, my dear long-time friend; they all
turned to look at me for a moment, hoping that I had managed to exert some influence through Chuza, my husband, but
Herod had only laughed at him. I shook my head and all hope
left their eyes.

Other women were surrounding us—so many had Jesus
blessed through those short months—old women and young,
married and single, many of them widowed, others having lost
sons, all of them acquainted with grief. And now we were all

joined in a sorrow unimaginable before this day. *If they kill the good man, what will happen to the rest?* I heard a mother cry out. The keening rose and ascended to the silent heavens, and for me his funeral was already taking place. We all joined in the mourning. Our dearest friend, our master and rabbi had been condemned like a prisoner and there was no hope left for any of us. We surged forward in such misery that even the Romans made way.

They paused for a little while and we, desperate, not thinking, ran to Jesus. He turned to us immediately and I saw tears gather in his eyes and spill on the ground. He looked at us with pity, but all of it was for us, not for himself. "Oh, daughters of Jerusalem," he said, and I knew he meant all of us there, and every woman going about her chores in the city, and everyone on the surrounding countryside. "Weep not for me," he told us, and we fell quiet, listening. He glanced briefly at the Romans, then at the men following them, and then he looked over the city he had loved, the city that had not loved him back. "Weep for yourselves and for your children," he said again, and I knew that in that uncanny way of his he was looking to the future, and the weight of an impending disaster overwhelmed me.

Someone cried, "We are weeping for you, Jesus. Comfort us as of old."

But he said, "Oh daughters of Jerusalem, the time is coming when you will bless the barren, and the wombs that never bore, and the breasts that never suckled a baby. . . ." We hushed then, and a terrible silence fell on the crowd. He asked in a voice that held all the world's sorrow in it, "If they do this when the wood is green, what will they do when it is dry?"

The Romans pushed us back. You could see a collective nervousness come upon them. They are a superstitious lot and they had heard his words. One of them lifted the whip but we all cried out, "No, enough! Let it fall on us."

Jesus turned to look at us one more time, saying his last good-bye to us, I think, and the most intense loneliness covered me. I learned later that the others felt the same—terribly alone and frightened.

We stayed back, and I heard a voice cry out, "Let the mountains fall on us to cover us."

"They have already done so," I replied, but Mary the Magdalene pulled me by the hand. "Come, Joanna," she said, "we must not let him be alone at this time. We must stay with him to the end."

"Yes," his mother whispered. "We will stay with him to the end. And then may we all die with him."

The rest of us agreed, we who had followed him during those exhilarating months of his doing good wherever he went. We would stay with him to the end, no matter what happened to us. And as we trudged on behind the sad procession, a strange calm came over me. I put his terrible last words from my mind and remembered another day when he had cried out, "If you lose your life for my sake, you will find it!" I turned to Mary, "Do you remember..." I started, and she answered immediately, "I remember. I remember. This is why I will not abandon him." And we continued the climb to Golgotha.

Let us pray:

Jesus of sorrows, we remember today all the women who have given their love to those who need it— mothers and sisters and wives and daughters, single women, and grandmothers.

We remember all the women who have mourned because of war, because of disaster, and death.

We thank you for their love, their prayers, and their tears and all the pain endured on behalf of others.

Comfort all those who mourn today. Sustain them in hope.

Kyrie eleison.

Christé eleison

Kyrie eleison.

STATION IX

Jesus Falls the Third Time

As seen by Judas Iscariot

Jesus Falls the Third Time

So when he had dipped the piece of bread, he gave it to Judas son of Simon Iscariot. After he received the piece of bread, Satan entered into him. Jesus said to him, "Do quickly what you are going to do." John 13:26b–27

While he was still speaking, suddenly a crowd came, and the one called Judas, one of the twelve, was leading them. He approached Jesus to kiss him; but Jesus said to him, "Judas, is it with a kiss that you are betraying the Son of Man?" Luke 22:47

hat possessed me? Who possessed me? Was it Satan as the Master said? How could I have done such an evil thing?

All I wanted for him was to succeed! Is that a bad thing? He had all the makings of a great leader, the true Messiah of the people of Israel, the only one who could lead us out of slavery to liberty. Up to this very moment I have been expecting him to change things.

But hiding down here at the bottom of the hill in the stink of Gehenna and all the refuse of Jerusalem, watching the procession above me, seeing the hated Romans push him uphill to his death, I have given up hope. After all those months of expectation, he didn't do what I had wanted so passionately—to take up arms and to rebel. I have finally accepted it. When a moment ago I saw him stumble and fall, when I watched him struggle to stand up and then take hold of the Roman's arm, I lost all hope. Here, in the stink and smoke of Gehenna, I scream alone. The end has come for me also.

He was such an attractive prospect. From the first moment, when I saw his strength—his leg muscles developed like those of a soldier, his shoulders broad and powerful—and then that face of his with the eyes that revealed such intelligence, courage, and wisdom, I was hooked. *Yes, Lord, this is the one you have promised us. He will lead us into freedom.* So gladly, almost giddily, I became one of his followers. How seductive it was to find an intelligent Jew, from Galilee of all places, who could match me wit for wit, whose countenance was shining with light from within. *This is the one,* I thought again and again, *this is the one! The end of the occupation is coming. He will lead us to victory.*

Later, when I watched him perform those miracles of his that won him so many followers, I knew them as signs of the Messiah and of the Jewish kingdom. He called it God's kingdom or the kingdom of heaven. Up to the very last, at that supper where he seemed so sad and so resigned, I thought, *This is it, this is the time of the kingdom.* Later, in the garden, when I moved up to kiss him, I knew that he would claim his kingdom, he would finally ask for a sword and, with me at his side, he would lead us to revolt. Instead he asked, "With a kiss you betray me, Judas?" Betray? I was not betraying him. I only wanted him to reveal himself for who he really was, is.

How could he let me down so? I never dreamt he would allow them to take him. His miracles had persuaded me that he would never let it happen. He could have called legions from heaven, I was convinced of that. Even he said it there in the garden—but that sad voice of his when he said it, how it cut me to the heart.

The rest of them were stupid Galileans, but he, he was the most intelligent man I have ever met. I was so sure he knew what I was all about. Again and again I gave him signals, but he didn't accept them; he refused to connect with the Zealots.

He has let them take him. He has let them defeat him. I was fooled after all. They will crucify him and end it all. There is nothing left for me but to follow him to the grave.

But oh, the bitterness of it. How sure I was of who he was, and how wrong I have been. Why did he do it? Why did he not listen to me? Five days ago, the whole city came out to welcome him. They were ready. All those Hosannas meant— "We are ready. Let's go after the Romans. You are the blessed one who comes in the name of the Lord. Let's go after them. You can lead us."

But he, instead of rushing in, came riding on a donkey. All my doubts, suppressed up to then, came to the surface. Was he a coward? He never before acted like one. Maybe he needed something drastic to make him change his mind. It was then I decided to go to the authorities, desperate to force his hand. To the very end, right there in the garden, I was sure he would come to himself and acknowledge who he is. Why didn't he do it? How could I have been so mistaken? How?

Ah, look, the procession has reached Golgotha. He is putting up no resistance. He wasn't the Messiah after all, and I have been a fool and a villain. I have betrayed a man who did nothing but good, yet one who had no ambition. There is nothing left to live for. Nothing for me to hope.

Let us pray:

Oh Jesus Christ, forgive us for trying to make you in our own image.

Again and again, like Judas, we have failed to recognize you.

Every idol that still lurks in our minds comes to the fore, and we think it is you, Lord Jesus.

Forgive us our sin.

Day after day we fashion you in our image by our words, our false loyalties, our lives.

Show us Jesus, the Son of Man.

Show us the glorified Christ.

Show us your true self.

Help us see the way of the cross as the way to life.

Kyrie eleison.

Christé eleison.

Kyrie eleison.

STATION X

Jesus Is Stripped of His Garments

As told by the gambling soldier

Jesus Is Stripped of His Garments

*When the soldiers had crucified Jesus they took his clothes
and divided them into four parts, one for each soldier.
They also took his tunic; now the tunic was seamless,
woven in one piece from the top. So they said to one
another, "Let us not tear it, but cast lots for it to see who
will get it." This was to fulfill what the scripture says,
"They divided my clothes among themselves and for my
clothing they cast lots." John 19:23–24*

 would gamble on anything and everything. Roman
pay was barely adequate for mere soldiers, and win-
ning at the dice was one way we had found to sup-
plement our salaries. We would toss for just about any extras
that came to mind. The higher-ups encouraged it. Knowing
what a thankless job it was to be on execution duty, they let us
roll the dice even for the clothes of the condemned.

Yeah, I know it's stupid and cruel, but what isn't, in this
mad world? Being far from home is bad enough. Most of the
time, the boredom of duty a vast sea away from home is
numbing. Those fancy historians, like Herodotus and Thucy-
dides, one day will write about us Romans. At least that's what
the learned Greek slaves who like my company tell me. They
will write what great warriors Caesar and Pompey, Augustus
and Tiberius were, but who will mention us, the poor foot soldiers who do all the fighting and the killing and the dying? Tell
me this, who will remember us?

And who will remember these other miserable dying ones
on the cross? Two of them are experienced criminals; they give
as well as they take. They have been cursing us from the hour

we tied them up, and they would have slit our throats had they
been given half a chance. But the third one, the quiet, dignified Jew who has all these women sobbing nearby, he has said
not one mean word to us. Stripping him of his clothes was so
easy, it made even me ashamed. We left his loin cloth in place,
just to save him a bit of dignity with his mother close by and
all these other women who haven't stopped weeping. But we
took the headdress, the tunic, the sandals and the zona, and
his bloodied cloak. The cloak we cut in narrow strips to tie
'round our own sore legs. I chose the zona; my buddy wanted
the sandals; he'll sell them to some poor traveler tomorrow,
I'm sure. And a third said laughing, "I'll have the headdress, to
show back home how funny these men's head covering is." He
put it on and we laughed with him; he was welcome to it. But
the tunic was of one whole cloth, no seams in it, a nice linen
piece that someone wove lovingly on her loom. It made me
feel weird all over touching it. Someone had loved him very
much. Which one of the women was it? We didn't want to
tear this one, so we tossed for it. We sang our ditties, noisy
and crude as always, until the centurion came to tell us to shut
up. "These are respectable women," he said, pointing to the
lamenting group, and I could tell the old soldier was shaken.

It surprised me. How many of these executions had he
supervised? It must be hundreds. What was it about this one?

We toned it down, tossed one more time, and I won the
tunic. I took it in my hands and then came close to throwing
it into the fire we had lit to warm the chilly air.

"What is it, man?" my buddy asked. "You're white as a
ghost."

"Not surprising," I answered. "A ghost just walked all over
me."

It was now very dark and cold, and we all thought it the
worst of omens. The middle of the day it was, and dark as
night. Ominous-like, the atmosphere shivered like the early
hints of an earthquake coming. Shaken, we stopped singing
and guffawing and grew fearful. In that trembling quiet I

heard a woman's voice pleading, "At least let me have his tunic, centurion. I will be glad to buy it back from the soldier. Only, I do think his mother ought to have it."

"Sir," I called out, trying to break the spell. "Sir, here it is. Let the mother have it." The centurion felt his way back to us, and said, "This is damned strange, men. Make sure nobody runs away and starts a tale that will frighten the populace. Stay alert and keep the order."

"Here, sir," I said again. "I heard a woman ask you for his tunic."

"That's right," he said, "but you won it fair and square. I wouldn't want to take it from you."

"Take it, take it," I said, and forced it into his hands, not wanting him to see how mine were trembling. "It's only fair for the mother to have it. It's good cloth. She must have spent days weaving it."

The centurion looked at me with puzzlement, and I saw him trembling as he touched it. He shook his head and looked to the dark skies. "More and more peculiar," he said. "I wonder who he is, though I'm afraid I know."

He shivered and I followed him as he approached the women. One of them, beautiful even in that half light, her head covered but her stricken face visible, reached out her hand for the seamless tunic. "Thank you, centurion," she said. "We will not forget this kindness and generosity."

The centurion, a fair man—the kind I would fight for—said to her: "It's not my doing, Mary of Magdala. This soldier won it, but he's giving it back to the grieving mother."

The woman then approached me, and I saw the tears still in her eyes, her lovely face ravaged with grief. "Soldier," she told me solemnly, "the one who wore it was the best man who ever lived. I thank you." And she disappeared into the dark and sorrow of the day.

I'm glad I gave it to her. How could I ever wear the tunic of the best man who ever lived? The terrors of this day are enough.

Let us pray:

Lord, the humiliation Jesus suffered reminds us of all
those who are humiliated daily at work, at home, at
school.

Have compassion upon them.

We remember those whose work is not honored; those
who have to stoop to degrading jobs that strip them
of their humanity in order to survive.

Give to them the dignity of love.

We pray for those who are homeless, who are abused,
who are dishonored.

*And we pray for their abusers, and for all of us who, for
reasons unknown to us, lose our humanity because of a
mean spirit.*

Restore to us the wholeness of creation.

Kyrie eleison.

Christé eleison.

Kyrie eleison.

STATION XI

Jesus Is Nailed to the Cross

As seen by the soldier on duty

Jesus Is Nailed to the Cross

Make the minds of these people dull,
and stop their ears,
and shut their eyes,
so that they may not look with
their eyes,
and listen with their ears,
and comprehend with their minds,
and turn and be healed.
Isaiah 6:10

he trick is not to look them in the eye. You drag them, you kick them, you crucify them, but you don't look them in the eye. If you slip up and look into their eyes, you can't do the job. You are here to do this job. So do it, but don't get involved.

I had learned my lesson well. When I first came to this land, I was young and ignorant and didn't pay attention to what the commander told us in training. "We don't crucify *Romans,*" he emphasized, "so you don't need to worry. You won't hurt anybody who matters. All these are slaves and criminals, but they are not Romans. Think of them in those words—slaves and criminals. We all know that Rome didn't get where she is by being soft. We have to show them who is strong. We have to show them who has the power, who is number one. So don't pity them. Show them who it was who brought them peace, the great Pax Romana."

I should have listened to the commander that first time. But I looked into the boy's eyes—that's what he was, a boy like me—and then I couldn't drive the nail. I froze. The other soldier on the detail wasn't squeamish. He'd done it before. So he lifted the hammer and drove the nail. I heard it tear through the flesh and the bones of the ankle, I heard the boy's scream rip the air around me, and I was deathly sick. The others laughed at me, and then they forced me to do it. Standing above my head, bent over as I was, they taunted me until I lifted the hammer and drove the nail through the hands. The boy turned one more time to look at me, his mouth open in a silent scream this time, and then he passed out. I wanted to do the same, but the other soldiers were watching me closely. It doesn't pay to be a coward and a Roman. So I obeyed orders. That's the second trick. Obey orders. Don't look them in the eye and obey orders. If you don't think of them as boys, or men, or Syrians, or Jews, or Germans, you can make it. Think of them as enemies, as slaves and prisoners, and you can do it.

Then it becomes routine. Like everything else, killing becomes routine. You get used to it. The more you do it, the easier it becomes.

I was on the job that spring day, when Pilate was still procurator of Judea. It was the time of the Jewish Passover, and that always meant trouble. It celebrated some memory they had of old, of victory, or some escape, I understand, and that gave them the courage they lacked at other times. So we were told to be on the watch. "Troublemakers, priests, and prophets," the commander sneered. "They cause the problems. So watch out. I hear there is one among them who is causing all kinds of furor and adulation. They told me he entered Jerusalem on the first day of the week and the crowd went wild. It was all connected with their strange symbolism. They said he rode in on a donkey, so I guess he's scared to appear to us like a rabble rouser. But the rest of it was weird. They covered the way with leafy branches, and some even spread their cloaks on the road. So be on the lookout. These Jews are ripe for revolt."

But they caught him early, and it seems that, after all, he had no followers. If he did before, they have disappeared already. No one challenged us. He seems to have had more women followers than men. Look around. These women are standing by, and I've got to hand it to them. They are weeping, but they don't flinch. A strange lot.

I am on the crucifixion detail. It's been a long time since I got sick from the thought of it. Like I said—you get used to anything if you do it often enough. And the trick is not to look them in the eye. I've been careful since that first time.

First, they told me to nail a sign on the cross—I can't read it, but someone said it means *Jesus of Nazareth King of the Jews.* Give it to us Romans—our sense of humor doesn't desert us. But I wish I hadn't learned his name. So I lifted the hammer to bring it down on the wrists, and it was at that moment I heard his voice. I was used to the cursing—that's the usual response, to curse us nonstop while they still have breath. But this one, this fake king, said not a word. "He's a quiet one," I said to my buddy, but he grunted, "You watch out for the quiet ones." And then the prisoner spoke in a voice that made me jump out of my skin, "When you think of this, my son, remember, I forgive you."

I pretended I hadn't heard because my insides started shaking. "Not again," I thought, "by Mars, not again." Habit kicked in, and I finished the job and managed not to look him in the eye.

But now, here in the dark, seeing the outline of the cross against the night sky, I sit and weep.

Let us pray:

Oh Christ Jesus, how many of us have driven nails in
   your hands without knowing we were doing so.

Have mercy on us.

Throughout the centuries, many of us, as obedient
   soldiers, have killed others while obeying orders.

Have mercy on us.

Many of us with our money, our vote, our will, our orders, our words have caused others to find untimely and violent deaths.

Forgive us, Lord.

As you forgave those who crucified you, we also ask for your forgiveness.

Kyrie eleison.

Christé eleison.

Kyrie eleison.

STATION XII

Jesus Dies on the Cross

As seen by the centurion

Jesus Dies on the Cross

*Then Jesus gave a loud cry and breathed his last. And
the curtain of the temple was torn in two, from top to
bottom. Now when the centurion who stood facing him
saw that in this way he breathed his last, he said, "Truly
this man was God's Son."* Mark 15:37–39

I've seen many people die, and this may be put on my
gravestone at my death: "A faithful servant of Rome,
he supervised the execution of a large number of
criminals." For a Roman centurion this is a fitting tribute. For
the man I am now, this is my condemnation.

You can't serve in Jerusalem and not know what's happening among the people. Pilate communicates only with the
high priests, but it is left to the centurion to know what the
people in the streets are saying. That's how we enforce order
and keep the peace. So, I was quite aware that this execution
was irregular, to state the obvious. I had never before been
involved in a trial so hasty, so hurried and furtive. I had never
been summoned in the middle of the night to be told to have
my soldiers ready, in front of the praetorium, at dawn. Something strange was happening, and I had no desire to be
involved in another mad scheme of Pilate's that would leave
the people furious with Rome and my soldiers in constant
danger of an impending uprising.

In the light of the torches I had a glimpse of the prisoner
as he was being led from Caiaphas' quarters to Pilate's praetorium. More and more curious. Caiaphas must have conferred
with Pilate overnight. Why the secrecy? My feelings of unease
increased. And as the prisoner passed by me, I glanced at his

impressive face. Something stirred within me—a memory, the words of a fellow centurion from Galilee, telling me a peculiar story when we met over a cup of brew recently. "My slave Demetrius was deathly sick, so I sent word to a local healer by the name of Jesus. I had been most impressed by the man's reputation; nothing of the charlatan clouded his name, nothing of the profiteer. From all reports, he sounded like a noble man. They had told me of his remarkable healing powers, and when I saw poor Demetrius on his deathbed, I felt pity for him—you remember how he had saved my life in the German wars—and I wanted this Jewish rabbi to heal him. I sent word, but asked him not to enter my house. I was afraid of so much power coming under my roof—what if he was from the gods after all?—but I also wanted to show respect to him and his people: Why should we Romans not show respect for the noble ones among the Jews? So I said to him, 'Teacher, I know both the meaning of power and of obedience. I say to my soldiers, *Go,* and they go. I say, *Come,* and they come. You have power over the forces of illness. So order this fever to depart from my slave.' And it was done. He seemed to be amazed that I, a Roman, had such respect for him. He looked at me with admiration, and I saw a smile on his face, but also a deep regret as he addressed his own people. It seems that they were not taking him as seriously as I had. A strange and wonderful encounter, indeed. I cannot get it out of my mind."

Now all these words of my comrade arose from my memory, and I thought, Is it possible? Is this the healer? Something in his bearing must have brought my comrade's words to mind. To this day, I don't know why I made the connection so quickly. There is something about a man that is unmistakable—integrity—the most distinct quality of all, and the prisoner possessed it. I asked the soldier nearest me about him, and the soldier in turn made inquiries among the Jews in the yard and came back to report to me: "The name of the prisoner is Jesus. He has a reputation as a healer and a great teacher. At the first of the week, he was hailed here as a liberator. But it seems the high priest is worried about so much power in a man who has no priestly title, so here is their Jesus today—standing before Pilate."

My foreboding increased. What had the man done? He didn't look like the usual Zealots and revolutionaries to me. I waited for Pilate's orders, but the trial was having its peculiar moments. Pilate, lately so ready to please the Jewish authorities—after his notorious fiasco—was vacillating. Why? He kept coming out to the portico, because the Jews refused to enter the Court of the Stranger: it would defile them before their Sabbath. After making his announcements to them, Pilate would return inside to confer with the prisoner. Every time he emerged he looked more and more puzzled. I would have given anything to have been in the hall, but my orders were to stand outside to prevent a riot. It seems the prisoner had a huge following among the people, but it was still early, and most of them were either asleep or hadn't heard the news of his arrest. Only his enemies seemed to be outside the palace.

The night was dragging on. Suddenly, I was summoned to accompany Jesus to Herod's Jerusalem palace, but that didn't last long. Back to Pilate we were sent, with the prisoner exhausted but retaining his enormous dignity throughout, his eyes clear but sad, his stark aloneness the most obvious memory of that strange night.

Early in the morning, Pilate made up his mind. The prisoner would be crucified. How I loathed the practice! But a Roman soldier is not supposed to have emotions, so I learned to obey the orders with the least fuss and to be quick about it. I arranged the procession in as orderly a fashion as the situation permitted me and we set out for Golgotha. There were moments on that walk that I will never forget, different from any I had encountered in the past, but it is the end of the whole sordid affair that concerns me here. It was when the prisoner Jesus drew his last breath.

There was an inscription above his cross that said, *Jesus of Nazareth King of the Jews,* the only blow Pilate forced on the Jews who were made furious by the words.

But I didn't think the words either funny or mocking. Jesus was a man of great spiritual refinement—this I could tell. Not a word of anger passed his lips; we were used to being cursed by those we executed. But he remained quiet, unbearably sad, withdrawn but alert, aware, as if he were communicating with someone the whole time, but I had no idea who that someone was until the very end.

He died earlier than most, and for that I felt a peculiar kind of gratitude. The agony on the cross is so extreme that nothing human remains in those who die and those who put them to death. He had been uttering some sounds and directing a few words to those who loved him and stood below weeping. I let them stay; everyone needs some comfort near the end. I too would like to die with a loved one near me. But when a great cry arose from deep within him, his last breath escaping, there was a word I recognized and I thought it was Greek—*tetelestai*—a word of utter finality, of accomplishment. What cosmic drama is ending? I wondered and shivered from head to toe. For the past three hours an unnatural darkness had fallen on that hill, and the sun seemed to disappear. We felt abandoned by the universe. Now, as he cried out the final cry that broke his heart, the sun appeared again. What does it all mean, I wondered as I trembled from a mystery that encircled me. I was feeling that something had ended and something was beginning that was beyond everyone's grasp. Had he been communicating with God until the very end?

Who was he? Who is he? I heard myself say aloud: "Truly this man was God's Son!" And I knew that this was different, utterly different from the title of Augustus who had been proclaimed a god at his death, something everyone said but no one in his right mind believed. But this one, this poor Jewish rabbi who bore his death as no one else, who thought of others until the very end, *his* death altered the universe. I will have to spend the rest of my days trying to understand it.

Let us pray:

Lord Jesus, you have revealed yourself even to those who don't know your name,

As you have revealed yourself to those who proclaim your name.

May we live and die in such a way that your name is honored throughout the world.

Open our hearts and eyes so that we may see the Christ in others.

May we speak, and live, and love in ways that honor your name as you always honored the name of your Father in heaven.

Kyrie eleison.

Christé eleison.

Kyrie eleison.

STATION XIII

*The Body of Jesus Is Placed
in the Arms of His Mother*

As spoken by Joseph of Arimathea

The Body of Jesus Is Placed in the Arms of His Mother

After these things, Joseph of Arimathea, who was a disciple of Jesus, though a secret one because of his fear of the Jews, asked Pilate to let him take away the body of Jesus. Pilate gave him permission; so he came and removed his body. John 19:38

And now the hour has come for me to show the kind of man God created me to be—a man of courage and of honor. I have spent too many months watching Jesus from afar, longing to know him better, to feed on his words. But each time I tried to show that I was his friend, the thought of the others stopped me. *What will the brothers say? How can I, a member of the Sanhedrin, associate with one who is fast becoming the focus of my colleagues' dislike and anger?* The fear of losing face kept me from following my heart.

I now despise myself for it, but it is too late. The one thing left for me to do is to see that his body does not remain on the cross for vultures to poke at, unburied and defiled. No one can fault me for this desire. It is written in the Law.

So I am making my way to Pilate's court. I tried to keep the brothers from condemning the man Jesus and failed. They and Pilate have succeeded, and now, if there is justice in heaven, we all carry the burden of the death of a righteous man—Roman and Jewish authorities alike. I do not know about the people. If Jesus was right, God deals more mercifully with the poor and with those who don't know the Law than with those who have the knowledge. So may God have mercy on my soul also.

As I walk rapidly to Pilate's quarters, I think of my poor village of Arimathea, and of how far I have left it behind with my increasing wealth and prestige in the council. I have been a proud man. But thinking of that righteous Jesus on the cross makes all my achievements and my wealth seem as dross. Why didn't I speak up earlier? Why didn't I try harder to keep that good young man from the cross? Regrets and questions trouble me. I have decided to act, and I refuse to back down.

I ask the sentry for immediate admittance, using the name *Jesus of Nazareth* as my reason for requesting a hearing from Pilate. I am summoned inside quickly, but the first words out of Pilate's mouth are: "No more on Jesus of Nazareth. I have suffered enough from my wife because of that name."

I am taken aback, but I remember my resolution and say in my most authoritative voice: "Your excellency, I have come to request something that will finally put an end to your concern with this name. I have come to ask for permission to bury Jesus."

"Unorthodox for criminals, is it not? Your own people claimed he was an impostor, someone who claimed to be the Son of God? Wasn't that their charge?"

I refuse to play games. "It is written in our law, sir, that it defiles the nation to leave the dead unburied. We must bury him on the day he died, we must do so immediately, before the Sabbath arrives. Jesus died quickly, and God was merciful in that. We must be equally merciful."

"It is rather quick, isn't it?" Pilate muses. "I must first make certain that he is dead indeed. Marius, go to the centurion on duty at the execution site and find out if the man is dead."

Marius is not long in returning and I am thankful, because Pilate and I have little to say to each other. An impressive older centurion enters with the slave. He verifies to Pilate that Jesus is dead. "It was a quick end, Pilate. The man died in a dignified manner, as he had lived, I understand. One of my soldiers, before I had a chance to forbid it, drew a sword and pierced his side. The way the blood seeped out sluggishly, without spurting, told us that he was already dead. I must confess that I was glad he did not suffer longer."

"Yes, yes," Pilate says quickly. "Everything about that young man seems to have been quite strange indeed. You may bury him according to your custom, Joseph, and pray don't let me hear any more from those priests of yours." He turns to leave. I thank him and depart immediately.

I own the space, a new grave cut in the rock above the quarry of Jerusalem, in a place we call Golgotha. There is a garden nearby and I had thought, since my home was far away, it would be a pleasant final resting place. I now want Jesus to be buried there. It is the least I can do, to honor him in this way.

I rush back to the place of execution together with the kind centurion. "Will it be possible," I ask him on the way, "to have some help in taking the body down from the cross?" He reassures me on that.

But when we arrive, we see women surrounding the cross. They are weeping uncontrollably. I say to them, "I have come to bury your Jesus. You may not want to be present when we take the body down. It is not a pleasant sight to see what the hanging from the nails does to a body."

An older woman, her face sad beyond human understanding, addresses me: "Kind sir, I will be grateful if you will let me stay. I need to hold him in my arms one more time."

How can I refuse? The centurion offers to do the work with his soldiers while I look after the women. Very gently, I move them aside, and the soldiers go about their grim business. A servant of mine is holding fresh bands of white linen, the shroud I have purchased for the occasion. We wrap the body up immediately, enough for the mother to hold him without seeing all the terrible wounds, and together we carry him to her as she sits on a rock. The other women form a circle around the two of them, the mourning mother and her dead son. She puts her arms around his body as one would hold a child and then a great wail arises from the depths of her being. "Ah, my son, my son, is there sorrow like unto my sorrow?"

There are no other words left to say.

Let us pray:

> For all who show mercy we offer thanks to you, oh God.
>
> *We recognize the Christ in those who respond to the needs of others in love and mercy.*
>
> For Joseph who buried the body of Jesus, we offer thanks.
>
> *For Mary, his mother, and all the women who ministered to Jesus, we offer thanks.*
>
> May we learn from their example, their loyalty, and courage to do your will no matter what the world expects of us.
>
> *Kyrie eleison.*
>
> *Christé eleison.*
>
> *Kyrie eleison.*

STATION XIV

Jesus Is Laid in the Tomb

As spoken by Nicodemus

Jesus Is Laid in the Tomb

*Nicodemus, who had at first come to Jesus by night, also
came, bringing a mixture of myrrh and aloes, weighing
about a hundred pounds. They took the body of Jesus and
wrapped it with the spices in linen cloths, according to
the burial custom of the Jews. Now there was a garden in
the place where he was crucified, and in the garden there
was a new tomb in which no one had ever been laid.
And so, because it was the Jewish day of Preparation,
and the tomb was nearby, they laid Jesus there.*
John 19:39–42

f Joseph can show courage, I should do the same. I
was the one who spent the most interesting night of
my life listening to the young rabbi, so full of wisdom and quick turns of mind he was, so full of surprises that
shook the foundation of a lifetime of thinking and studying!

I had gone to him in the night—the fear of what others
might make of our actions is never far from our minds—and
he answered my questions in the most unexpected ways imag-
inable. I was so attracted to that mind, so impressed by the
shining integrity of his person, the deep piety mixed with
humor, the ability to look beyond words into the essence of
thought, the delightful way he had with stories and parables.
Why couldn't I have been open about my admiration? What
kept me from joining his followers? Questions I must ponder
the rest of my life, though I'm afraid I can guess at the answers.

And now, here I am, grieving together with Joseph and
Jesus' closest friends. I see they are mostly women, and I wonder if his male disciples are like me—afraid, hiding in the dark

places. It matters not. This is not an atmosphere that allows for courage. He had it, the young rabbi Jesus, he was the essence of courage and integrity. But look where it brought him: to the disgrace, the scandal of the cross. How do I deal with this reality? Is this God's punishment or man's? If the truth dwelled in Jesus, why did God punish him? On the other hand, if the truth dwelled in Jesus, I can understand why Pilate and Caiaphas would not be able to face it or endure it. We do have a habit of destroying truth tellers. I must think on this later.

But now, now finally I must act. A servant of Joseph's came a few hours ago to tell me that a tomb was prepared for the body of Jesus. Would I be willing to help with the burial?

My house is full of spices and herbs. The moment I heard of the decision to crucify him I sent my servant to buy them in profusion—aloe, camphor, labdanum, nard, oil of cedar, cloves, frankincense, and myrrh . . . he will be buried like a king, for a king he was indeed.

I see Joseph has taken the body down from the cross. I am glad to hear that Jesus' legs did not have to be broken to hasten death before the Sabbath. He lies now in the arms of his mother, and a sorrow beyond knowing engulfs all who surround them.

"Joseph, the time has come, we must hurry in order not to violate the Sabbath."

Joseph nods at me. Very gently he asks the mother for the body of her son. Quietly now, with no tears, she touches the face of her beloved, and Joseph and I, assisted by our servants, lift the lifeless body and carry it across the garden to the tomb.

Joseph has done very well. It is a fine cave indeed in surroundings that speak of peace and beauty. I smell the pines, the lilies that are blooming on this spring evening. The birds utter a few trills and then fall quiet. It is still now; nothing moves. The atmosphere, so ominous a few hours ago, is benign. Has the great struggle ceased?

We enter the tomb, only Joseph and I. The servants stand respectfully outside. There is a large slab of stone in the center of the cave, and on it we lay the body and I sprinkle profuse spices on it. Then the two of us wind the long sheet around and around the body until everything is covered in white. His pierced brow has stopped bleeding, but I can still see the marks of the thorns. Tenderly, I lift the head and Joseph winds a separate long white band around it. That winsome face is covered now. Only the memory of his goodness and laughter remain.

We exit walking backwards, as if in the presence of a king. The stone on the side of the cave is round and flat and looks extremely heavy. The four of us put our weight and strength to it, and slowly, with great difficulty, we seal the tomb.

As we leave quietly I get a glimpse of movement behind those bushes, across from the tomb. Ah, Mary of Magdala is watching. There is another woman with her, but I don't recognize her. Poor Mary. How difficult it must be for these women who loved him to see all that energy snuffed out, all that love suppressed and the flame put out.

I pretend I do not see them. I pray that they find some comfort in knowing that we honored his body.

I go home to celebrate the Sabbath, but my heart is heavy. What will the new day bring? What has happened to all the hopes of those who loved him? What does it mean to die, to cease to exist? And what did he mean about being born again? Jesus, where is the new life you promised?

Let us pray:

Lord Jesus, we stand in fear before you.

We have not always shown courage in proclaiming your name. Like Nicodemus, we have been afraid to proclaim our love and loyalty.

Have mercy on us and forgive us.

Kyrie eleison.

Christé eleison.

Kyrie eleison.

On this last station fill us with the promise of the empty tomb.

On this last station fill us with the knowledge that life that does not end here.

For all who grieve we pray for comfort and for strength.

For all who grieve we pray for the assurance of the resurrection.

Kyrie eleison.

Christé eleison.

Kyrie eleison.